CREDIT RIVER VALLEY

CREDIT RIVER VALLEY

Credit Valley Conservation Foundation — Photographs by John de Visser

Stoddart

A BOSTON MILLS PRESS BOOK

Canadian Cataloguing in Publication Data

De Visser, John 1930-
 Credit River Valley

ISBN 1-55046-072-2

1. Credit River Valley (Ont.) – Pictorial works.
I. Credit Valley Conservation Foundation.
II. Title.

FC3095.C7D38 1992   971.3′53504′0222
F1059.C7D38 1992   C92-095109-0

Foundation Members: Lou Parsons, Glen Schnarr, Joan Breen, Russ Cooper,
Rick Winter, Barbara Siskind, Harold Kennedy
Special thanks to: Vicki Barron, Robert Peace

Edited by Noel Hudson
Design by Gillian Stead
Typography by Justified Type Inc., Guelph, Ontario
Printed and bound in Hong Kong by BookArt Inc.

First published in 1992 by
Stoddart Publishing Co. Limited
34 Lesmill Road
Toronto, Canada
M3B 2T6

A BOSTON MILLS PRESS BOOK
The Boston Mills Press
132 Main Street
Erin, Ontario
N0B 1T0

Winners of the
Heritage Canada
Communications Award

American Association
for State and Local History
Award Winner

OVERLEAF: *The Lower Credit at Burnhamthorpe.*

The Credit Valley Conservation Foundation
wishes to acknowledge the major funding contribution
of the following companies
without whose support
this pictorial tribute to the Credit River Valley
would not have been possible.

H.U.M.E. FOUNDATION

Established 1975
Jerry Humeniuk & R.B.Humeniuk
Founders

Lake view.

Contents

LAKE ONTARIO

Drawn by John Haines from the Halton-Peel Tapestry Map.
Copyright 1987 Tapestry Graphics Inc.

FOREWORD

Formed in December 1964, the Credit Valley Conservation Foundation's overall objective is to aid the Credit Valley Conservation Authority in the cultivation and advancement of conservation.

The Credit Valley Watershed is undeniably one of the most beautiful and diverse watershed's in Ontario.

Contributing greatly to the beauty and quality of the watershed are its wetlands. Yet population growth, agriculture and development activities have consumed vast acres of southern Ontario's wetlands. The ecosystem of the Credit Valley watershed relies on healthy wetlands for ecological, hydrological and recreational functions.

For this reason, the Credit Valley Conservation Foundation in co-operation with its generous sponsors, seek your support.

Proceeds from the sale of this book will go towards the purchase and maintenance of wetlands in the Credit Valley watershed.

We hope you enjoy the Credit River Valley and take the time to visit the many wonderful places so gloriously depicted within these pages.

Lou Parsons
Chairman
Credit Valley Conservation Foundation

Orangeville Reservoir.

INTRODUCTION

From its headwaters in Mono and East Garafraxa townships, the Credit River flows south to Lake Ontario, its watershed covering some 1,070 square kilometres. This watershed has experienced dynamic geological stresses, witnessed important historical events and been the subject of environmental concerns. The Credit is a river of contrasts — flowing from the western Ontario uplands to the St. Lawrence lowlands, from quiet rural countryside to energetic urban centres. It is a river of curiosities, and a river which possesses ineffable, intangible qualities that have nothing to do with environmental, historical or geological data.

With this book the Credit Valley Conservation Foundation hopes to heighten your knowledge of the Credit River Valley and to leave you with an intimate appreciation of its beauty and importance. It is only through this kind of knowledge and appreciation that we can effect any type of conservation — and the Credit River Valley *is* worthy of conservation.

Our journey through time and place starts in the Credit River's headwaters and ends at its mouth. We begin about 500 million years ago, during the Ordovician geologic period, when the Earth was undergoing enormous physical changes. Sedimentary shales were being deposited on ancient sea beds, deposits that can now be recognized in the red Queenston shales evident at Church's Falls (The Cataract) and Terra Cotta. Later, during the Silurian period, vast shallow and warm inland seas spread across much of the area, providing ideal breeding conditions for flourishing aquatic life. Sediments carried into these seas by rivers created layers of sandstone, and over these fell layers of limestone and harder dolomite (composed largely of

magnesium and calcium carbonates, the result of decaying animal and plant matter). These layers of sedimentary strata accumulated until the Silurian seas retreated.

Around this time the entire area warped when western Ontario lifted into a broad dome known as a geoanticline. The Credit Valley now lies on the eastern slope of the dome. The rise in altitude to the west becomes dramatic where the Niagara Escarpment passes through the watershed.

With the exception of the Niagara Escarpment, most of the area would have been monotonously flat after the retreat of the Silurian seas. Enter the glaciers. These massive earth-movers scoured, scraped, shoved and dumped material in an almost organized fashion. As they retreated, meltwaters formed enormous rivers that ran along spillways still in existence. The Credit River occupies a connected spillway system as far down as Glen Williams; the West Branch also follows a spillway. These raging watercourses created broad troughs bordered by gravel terraces that today support cedar swamps in their coarse, poorly drained soils.

Carrying enormous loads, the glaciers moulded deposits known as kame moraines, easily identifiable in the rolling Caldwell Sandy Hills and the Orangeville Sandy Hills, where the headwaters of the main branch of the Credit rise. Further south, in the Caledon Moraine, the deposit composition is coarser, often containing boulders of considerable size. Both types of moraine are characterized by wet valleys that support abundant wildlife. West of the Orangeville Sandy Hills, near Erin, the glaciers dropped whale-backed hills of richer soils, drumlin fields, through which numerous interconnecting valleys now weave.

Credit River near Caledon.

Caledon Village parade.

Below the Escarpment the formation of the land took on a different dynamic. Influenced by both glacial lakes and rivers, here was formed an area of broad, fertile plains known as the Peel Till Plains, Shale Plain and Port Credit Sandy Plain, interrupted only by the Streetsville Moraine, which is a gentle version of its northern cousins.

It is important to understand the geology of the watershed and how it affects not only the land's ability to support substantial flora but also its direct affect upon climate.

Essentially, in terms of climate, the watershed can be divided into three regions, that of the lakeshore, the Peel Plain and the uplands, with cooler, wetter weather occurring in the uplands, a moderate range on the Peel Plain and a mild influence toward the lake.

Life in and along the Credit flourishes because of these two factors, geology and climate, factors which played an important role in early settlement and later in the region's environmental problems.

Port Credit Yacht Club.

Main Street windows, Orangeville.

SETTLEMENTS AT THE HEADWATERS

Four kilometres northeast of Orangeville a river begins. It is an unspectacular beginning partially altered by development around the Orangeville Reservoir. Before the creation of the reservoir, there was a natural lake, Islands Lake, and a rather extensive cedar bog, from which flowed a feed stream that ran into Monora Creek, and from there into the Credit River and on to Lake Ontario.

The settlement of Orangeville began around 1844, when Orange Lawrence breezed into the backwoods. Although he wasn't the first settler — that title goes to Ezekiel Benson, a land surveyor — Orange Lawrence had the stuff to make a town happen.

By 1851 he had Chisholm Miller draft the first town plan, which laid out the lower half of the south side of the present town. Here Lawrence built a tavern and store. He also purchased all the lands along the creek, developed several mills and sold off additional lands to settlers interested in developing their own mills. In 1857 he sold the site of present-day Watt's flour mill to Thomas Jull and John W. Reid, who together built the first flour mill and later a sawmill. The flour mill continued in operation until 1972.

Another mill was established on the site of what is now Bailie Printing, and a carding mill, which later burned, was erected on Bythia. The oldest surviving building in town, the site of Greystones, was once a tavern run by Orange Lawrence.

As the settlement grew and flourished, plans were needed for the north side of town, and in 1856 planner J. Staughton Dennis was retained. Unlike the south side, with its narrow European-style streets, the north end was developed with broad roadways. By 1863 the community had grown

substantially enough that its denizens incorporated, naming the town in honour of its founder, Orange Lawrence.

Over the decades Orangeville continued to grow, becoming a dormitory town for a period. With the boom in housing came the need for a water treatment facility, and so the Credit River's headwaters were dammed in order to assure water quality and flow further downstream. In 1967 dams were constructed at the northern and southern exits from the marsh, preventing any drainage to the north, with the southern exit acting as a control gate. This damming flooded the wetlands. The existing lake extended, forming a shallow body with an average depth of 1.5 metres, its deepest section running to 7.5 metres. This allowed levels in the Credit to be controlled, ensuring enough capacity for the treatment facility. Orangeville Reservoir now provides haven for a considerable fish population as well as roosts for birds, including such species as mergansers and green herons.

Unlike so many mill towns, Orangeville has never suffered a substantial decline. Today it is the Dufferin County seat and a popular tourist destination.

Further to the south the Credit River swells from the entry of Shaw's Creek, another headwater stream. There is evidence that the Ojibwa once used this section of the Credit as part of a route from Lake Ontario to the Bruce Peninsula. Later the Europeans arrived, and it was here, along Shaw's Creek, that the village of Alton found its roots. The first European to settle the area was Thomas Russel Esq., in 1834, but just who named the village Alton is unclear.

William McClellan built the first sawmill in 1840, attracted by the speed of Shaw's Creek. In that same year grist and

Storm clouds gather northwest of Hillsburgh.

chopping mills were established by the Wright brothers on the 3rd Line. The Upper Mill came into existence in 1845 and produced yarns and blankets. This mill was later purchased by John M. Dodds, who moved his establishment to Orangeville in the 1930s. The building still stands.

With the establishment of these mills, the rails soon found reason to stop here. The Toronto, Grey & Bruce line and the Credit Valley line both made Alton part of their routes. As a result, the village opened up to other trades. A carriage-maker prospered here, as did several lime quarries, one of which was adjacent the Toronto, Grey & Bruce Railway at the far eastern end of town. The remains of a lime kiln, as well as a boarding house, can still be seen.

By 1850 the first church had been built. It was Methodist, as were so many towns' first churches. The Dixie House hotel was built by Archie Dick in 1870 at the corner of present-day Queen and Main. It was destroyed by fire in 1890 but rebuilt and renamed Palmer House. Another hotel, the Rockview or Rock Inn, went up at the east end of 2nd Line, adjacent the old Toronto, Grey & Bruce rail depot. It, too, was destroyed by fire, but never rebuilt. Fire was a constant danger in early Ontario communities. The school and two more hotels were consumed by fire. The school, however, was rebuilt in 1875 and is still in operation.

As if fires weren't enough, the village was flooded in 1889 when the McClelland dam broke and almost 3 hectares of water gushed down into the lower pond, smashing five dams. The force of the flood was so great that a 4-tonne boulder was moved 46 metres and damage exceeded that of Hurricane Hazel. This wasn't Alton's only flood. Several times, swollen from incessant rain or spring melts, Shaw's Creek spilled over its banks and rushed into the village.

Disasters in Alton weren't confined to fires and floods. In 1920 a meteor plunged into one of the millponds, boiling the water and rendering it too hot to swim.

Along yet another major tributary of the Credit, the West Credit River, sometimes called the Erin Branch, two other communities developed. The first of these was Hillsburgh. It began as most towns did, with a series of farms and a mill. Nathaniel Roszel was first to settle here, in 1820, after receiving a land grant for his services in the War of 1812. He was followed by William and Mary Howe of Kent, England,

and later by Aaron Wheeler and George Henshaw.

It was the enterprising Aaron Wheeler who guaranteed the mill-seat's security on what was to become the northeast block of town, in fact where the present arena stands. Wheeler established a grist mill. Later, Hiram Hill and his son Nazareth erected the settlement's first sawmill on Hiram's property.

By the 1850s a corduroy road to the area had been constructed. Hillsburgh grew and soon supported three tailors, a cooperage, a post office, several hotels, churches, general stores, doctors, a carriage works and a tanner.

Further downstream from Hillsburgh is Erin, established around 1832 when Daniel McMillan cleared 1¼ hectares for a sawmill southwest of the present post office. Many of the pines in the area were over 1¼ metres in diameter, and with this seemingly endless virgin forest, McMillan must have thought that his wealth was guaranteed. Two years later he built his first home, which was followed by a grist mill built with stone from Shingler's Limestone Quarry nearby.

By 1838 McMillan was doing so well that he raised a second sawmill. An oat mill followed, on the other side of the road. It was powered by a race from the lower dam. No respectable sawmill could do without a drying kiln, so one was constructed, and its ruins are still in existence. A second grist mill was built at the upper dam in 1840. Ten years later it was converted into a woollen mill.

All of this milling made for thirsty work, and William Cormack, enterprising man that he was, arrived in 1838 and established a distillery. Cormack was assured a supply of grain, as farmers who took their grain to the flour mill could have their tailings bagged separately and exchange them for Cormack's whisky. It is reported that farmers often had their jugs filled while waiting for their flour — much to the chagrin of their wives, no doubt. This distillery ran until 1860.

McMillan continued to expand and he soon established a cooperage. He built a fine residence in 1846, which twenty years later he sold to William Chisholm, receiving a hotel in the transaction.

While most of Erin's mills are gone, their races are still in existence, some of them continuing to run under the main street. One race remains in use at the local lumber supply store, and periodically the proprietor uses the old machinery to cut his wood.

Misty morning at Orangeville.

Orangeville tourist information caboose.

Orangeville war monument.

Orangeville Raceway.

At the post, Orangeville Raceway.

Golden fields, Orangeville.

The West Credit River southwest of Orangeville.

Reflections, Millcroft Inn, Alton.

Alton Mill Dam.

Fall birds near Hillsburgh.

Crossroads, East Garafraxa.

Snow dunes and earth, Erin Township.

Along the Erin 12th sideroad.

Erin Village on the West Credit.

Summer fun, Erin.

Mundell's old water-driven sawmill, Erin.

Old mill, Erin.

Big Al, farm near Erin.

Sheep Focus, Erin.

West Credit near Erin.

Sunrise, Erin Township.

The Niagara Escarpment near the Forks of the Credit.

FORKS OF THE CREDIT

The confluence where the West Credit meets the Credit proper is neither grand nor spectacular, but there is an ineffable quality about the Forks that has been the subject of much photography and painting. It is also an area with an interesting history, filled with legends and with the tales of early European settlers.

As happened in so many regions, gold fever also struck the Credit Valley. According to legend, there was an old native who regularly visited a local Scottish family, to whom he often displayed gold nuggets. To show his gratitude to the family for their many kindnesses, he promised to take their son to his secret place. The mother, alarmed at the idea of her son going alone with the native, had the father follow the two men. The father trailed them to an underground passage, but the trek failed there when the native disappeared between two rocks. The secret of the gold vanished with him.

This legend prompted a gold rush along the Credit around 1837. An estimated forty percent of the eager prospectors died before ever reaching the Credit Valley. Two men fell into deep caves and perished. Many of the prospectors who did reach the mining camp suffered from scurvy. And no gold was ever found. Only the legend remains.

Rail fever replaced gold fever. Two railways once steamed through the Credit Valley: the Credit Valley Railway and the Toronto, Grey & Bruce Line, the latter of which was narrow gauge. To construct a railway through this rugged country was no easy task. To reach the top of the Escarpment required a climb of 117 metres in 9 kilometres.

However, there is nothing that says enterprise must be this difficult. Back in 1910 J.J. McLaughlin knew the Credit Hills were filled with springs, and being a man with an eye for profit, he purchased 40 hectares on both sides of the CPR tracks, on the west bank of the West Credit River. He then established a company known as White Mountain Spring Water, also known as McLaughlin-Hygea Waters, bottled the water and sold it. With low overhead and good supply, McLaughlin did very well. His company went on to become known as Canada Dry, his first soft drink being Canada Dry Ginger Ale. Although the Credit Valley division of the company was closed in 1920, trucks are still periodically seen at the spring, filling their tanks with fresh water for both Canada Dry and Crystal Springs Water.

William Grant came to the Credit Valley in search of gold but instead came upon a salt spring frequented by deer. Excited by the discovery, he convinced his employer in York to underwrite an expedition. As a result of this expedition, the village of Gleniffer was established, complete with a sawmill and shacks. The salt, however, was buried too deep within the hills to justify its extraction, and the village was soon abandoned.

In 1858 Richard Church purchased Gleniffer for $100 and renamed it Church's Falls, with the dream of making it self-sufficient. When the railway came through, the people of the resurrected village renamed their community Cataract to avoid confusion with Churchville to the south. At the village's height, there were saw, grist and woollen mills, a stave and barrel plant, a broom factory and a brewery (which closed in 1865). What is now the Cataract Inn was formerly known as the Horseshoe Inn, built in 1855. It is

The Forks of the Credit, where the West Credit River meets the main branch.

one of the few remaining buildings from Cataract's early days. The church on William Street was built around 1890 and is now a private home which has been designated a historic site.

The northern entrance to the Forks of the Credit Provincial Park is also located in the village of Cataract. A Niagara Escarpment Natural Environment park, Forks of the Credit offers outstanding historic and natural features on 282 hectares. There is hope that the Ministry of Natural Resources will be able to procure an additional 65 hectares for the purposes of erosion control and environmental protection. This is a remarkable park in that a visitor is able to hike from Cataract down to the hamlet of Brimstone without ever having to leave the park. Plans are in the works to extend the trail system, allowing the hiker to wander all the way to the village of Belfountain.

The lakes within the Forks of the Credit Provincial Park are kettle lakes formed during the last glaciation. In the upper area, not far from Cataract, are Church's Falls and the remains of a hydro operation. If you look beneath the falls, you will see the area that was quarried of stone for the sawmill that later became Wheeler Brothers.

In 1890 John Deagle purchased the burned-out Wheeler Brothers mill for $1,800 and used it for a time as a grist mill. A clever man — the inventor of the spinning-tub washing machine — Deagle realized that competition would devour his meagre profits and in 1892 he converted the mill to a power plant. He was successful, coming on line at Cataract in 1899. Ten years later, the town of Erin was one of his customers. The business expanded so that by 1928 his system supplied Hillsburgh, Forks of the Credit, Brimstone, Belfountain, Caledon Village, Inglewood, Cheltenham, Caledon East, and the townships of Caledon and Chinguacousy. He eventually sold the business to Ontario Hydro, which closed the operation in 1946 and dynamited the buildings in 1953. Cataract Lake is now gone, leaving only hulking cement walls and the ruins.

Further downstream, toward Belfountain, the character of the river changes. Perhaps one of the most inspiring times to visit is in the spring, when the Credit breathes mist, and deadfall in the river transforms into wading dragons. The trails here are extensive and well worth a day of hiking. Fishing is allowed, as there are excellent stocks of brook and brown trout. In fact, the Credit supports one of Ontario's best trout fisheries.

The fishery can essentially be divided into two sectors, the upper and lower, the upper consisting of the Credit River

headwaters and tributaries to Inglewood in the south, and the lower from Inglewood to Lake Ontario.

Historically the Credit was always generous with its gifts of fish. For centuries native tribes included the Credit's fish as part of their basic diet. But the Europeans swarmed to the New World and brought with them their industrial practices. The fish were harvested on a massive scale, the land relieved of its overabundant forest, the Credit dammed and dammed again to turn the wheels of industry. This savage country and her savage people would be brought into order. It had been the way in Europe for time beyond the immigrants' reckoning, and so, to them, this land of almost obscene bounty was nothing less than chaos. What none of these people realized was that there was already in existence an older order, an infinitely more complex and efficient order than anything they could imagine.

As the forests fell, the soils silted into the Credit. As the soils silted the river, the fish died. As the dams followed one upon the other, the river level dropped, warming the cooler upper region and making it an inhospitable habitat for coldwater species like trout. As forest and vegetation cover was stripped from the Credit's banks, shaded areas disappeared as havens for fish and wildlife. The accumulated silt also smothered much of the insect life essential for the fishes' survival. As mills churned out flour, lumber and cloth, effluent spewed into the Credit, robbing it of oxygen and muddying the waters.

The glory days of fish from bank to bank were gone. Yet our ancestors continued these practices into the 20th century. Without forest cover and perceived chaos to hinder expansion, they built other industries along the Credit's banks, thinking to utilize all this fresh water for manufacturing processes. Mills — now expanded to include paper — dumped chlorine, mercury and a lethal combination of other contaminants into the watercourse. Tanneries joined them. Municipalities saw the Credit as a solution to their sewage problems, at first admitting raw sewage and later treated effluent.

As a species, we are learning — slowly, but learning. The most important lesson we've learned is that we can no longer continue a parasitic relationship with our planet. A benevolent symbiosis is infinitely preferable, recognizing that we are not above the fabric of nature, but rather one of the most dynamic and destructive forces in it. We can also be one of the most creatively constructive forces. It is this creativity that is required if we and other species are to survive.

We now know that some species of fish are indicator species. That is, they are like environmental barometers,

The Ministry of Natural Resources and Credit Valley Conservation Authority fishery crews "electro fishing" along the Credit. A harmless shock is sent through the water, bringing fish to the surface for counting and analysis. Collecting data is important to fisheries management.

warning us of poor water quality and damage to surrounding habitat. Brook trout, once found throughout the watershed, is one such species. Requiring cool temperatures, lots of ground water, and plant cover on the river's banks, the brook trout is now confined to those parts of the watershed above the Escarpment. The removal of forest cover and the interruption of supplies of cold ground water to streams were major contributing factors to the brook trout's relocation.

In more recent times, co-operation between the Ministry of Natural Resources, the Credit Valley Conservation Authority and local fishing clubs has returned fish to many parts of the river, and populations of both native brook trout and brown trout, which is European in origin, have increased to unprecedented levels. The encouragement of catch-and-release fishing techniques, and landowners who realized that what they did on the land affected the fish in the river, have contributed to these successes.

The new-found health of the river, which supports the previously stocked but now self-sustaining populations of brook, brown and rainbow trout, gave biologists the courage to attempt to reintroduce the legendary Atlantic salmon.

Late in the summer of 1990 something happened that hadn't happened in over 100 years. An Atlantic salmon returned to the Credit River to spawn. Stocked in 1988 near Inglewood as a yearling, this historic fish returned to the waters it instinctively remembered, in a valiant attempt to pass its genes on to a new generation. With its return was also returned the hope of restoring part of the river's heritage once thought lost forever.

The success of the fishery hinges upon all of us realizing a change of perspective. Is a plant a weed or a haven for damsel flies hanging over the river? Given our climate, is it natural for a lawn to be green six months of the year, or only in spring and fall? Is that raggedy old tree an eyesore or a sunscreen providing a cool patch of water for some lurking trout? Beauty doesn't necessarily mean manicured gardens and tailored landscapes. Beauty can be found in a gnarled tree, in a river bank covered with spring wildflowers, in the wildlife that can be attracted to our own backyards if we just leave nature alone and remember that for each of our actions there may be an equal and opposite reaction.

Chilly waters at the Cataract.

Old power dam at the Cataract.

Putting on the storms at the Cataract Inn.

Rail trestle at the Cataract.

In Belfountain Conservation Area.

BELFOUNTAIN AND THE QUARRIES

Like so many frontier villages along the Credit, Belfountain formed around rapid water and a determined man, in this case around a man known as "Grize" McCurdy. Although McCurdy wasn't the first to settle here — that was William Frank, who built a dam and grist mill on the West Credit River and later sold it to Grize — for many years he dominated the settlement then known as, what else, McCurdy's Village.

Credit Valley gold fever had seized many men, but Grize fell victim to silver fever. He had a silver mine east of Belfountain and west of the Forks of the Credit, near Devil's Pulpit. Later a group of miners began a shaft for a silver mine in a depression known as Hogg's Hollow. That either Grize or the other miners actually found silver seems unlikely, as silver, like gold, isn't found in sedimentary rock. What these men probably found were minute quantities of lead, which has a fresh, silvery appearance when first cut.

The general store on the corner of Main and Bush streets was the first tavern, known as the Glover Tavern. Grize, a teetotaller, refused to sell land to Glover for his drinking establishment. Despite Grize's rejection, Glover managed to purchase the parcel on the corner of Main and Bush, and there he raised his building. When construction was completed, villager William MacDonald climbed the rafters, broke a bottle of whisky over the beams and proclaimed:

And so this building, it did rise,
Independent of Old Grize.
The old miser wouldn't sell,
So let him go plumb to hell.

Between the Credit and Mill Street (River Road), near the grist mill, Grize built his sawmill. It was agreed that he would rent it to Quaker Bull, but the transaction was to end in disaster. The two men argued about rent. In a fit of temper, Grize hit Quaker Bull. Much to Grize's surprise, the Quaker retaliated by striking him with an implement. This single blow sent Grize to the ground, where he hit his head on a stone and died.

The village carried on, however, expanding to include several quarries, mills and a tannery — all the enterprises of a healthy centre.

It was a cooper named McNaughton who provided the tag of Tubtown to McCurdy's Village. To advertise his tub-making business, McNaughton erected a 3.5-metre-diameter tub-like building, much to the horror of his neighbours. When McNaughton left for Erin, the label Tubtown remained. The name Belfountain didn't come into existence until sometime between 1852 and 1857, seen on maps as Bellefountain. Over the years the spelling was shortened to Belfountain.

Summer swim, Belfountain.

The Belfountain Conservation Area is operated by the Credit Valley Conservation Authority. This Conservation Area has a curious history. In 1908 Charles W. Mack, a wealthy manufacturer of rubber stamps, purchased a strip of land along the Credit River for his retreat. He erected a cottage called Luck-e-nuf for himself and his family, and later another twelve-person guest house called Bide-a-wee. During his stay, the lands were cleared and the existing fountain and bell were constructed as symbols of the village. He also had created a mini-Niagara Falls with swinging bridge, several picnic and swimming areas, and lookouts. But scandal was to hound Mack, as it seems he offered his retreat to "unfortunate and under-priviliged" young women from his rubber stamp company. One of these women reportedly became pregnant and had an illegal abortion.

Carl Uteck purchased the property in 1946 and William Gress Rogers later bought it from Uteck. Rogers owned the lands until 1959, when the Credit Valley Conservation Authority acquired them. The Authority continued to add lands until 1973. Under the CVCA, cottages and buildings were demolished and facilities were improved.

The 12-hectare Belfountain Conservation Area offers fishing, nature trails, picnic areas and washrooms. It is a delightful place to spend an afternoon.

One of the Credit Valley's great attractions is a high wall of dolomite known as Devil's Pulpit. When viewed from the correct vantage point it does look like a pulpit, but why this spectacular natural feature was associated with the devil remains a mystery.

With the economic boom brought by the railways, communities felt the need to erect buildings of permanence and dignity, thus the area's quarries fared very well. During the late 1800s and early 1900s, the area around the forks became a frenetic centre of quarrying. Many of the quarries were owned by fortune-seeking lawyers. One and a half kilometres below the forks, on the 2nd Line, the first quarry was started to carve rock from the Escarpment. Number Two quarry, established by an Orangeville lawyer, ran only 137 metres east of Number Three quarry, known as York's Quarry. Both operated on the 3rd Line south of the forks. This quarry dug under the mountain. The Crow's Nest quarry encompassed three sites, and Number Five was in fact four quarries. These quarries provided the stone for Queen's Park buildings and the old Toronto City Hall.

By 1890 Carrol and Vick Company of Toronto had bought most the area's quarries. Bent on improving and expanding its holdings, the company built a lime and brick kiln with a towering chimney. But down drafts in the chimney thwarted this enterprise and three years later the kilns were closed.

In 1914 two fellows known as Proctor and McKnight decided that the clay deposits of the Escarpment could be used for profit, and to that end they established the Credit Tile and Brick Company, then located where the Caledon Ski Club now stands. The advent of concrete left them with an obsolete operation, and in the 1930s the brickworks closed.

The Caledon Ski Club came into existence as a result of efforts by Ross and Helen Wortley. In 1958 the Wortleys put in a rope tow outside of their home in Inglewood. In 1960 they purchased the present Caledon Ski Club property in the Credit hills with the intention of building a private ski area, which they did. By 1962, however, due to the need for capital to fund expansion of lodge facilities and snowmaking equipment, ownership passed from the Wortleys to the ski club members.

Today the Caledon Ski Club encompasses 73 hectares of prime wooded hills and valleys, of which eighteen hills are served by three chair lifts and three T-bars, and two beginner hills are served by surface lifts.

West Credit at Belfountain.

The Trimbles at Belfountain.

CREDIT VALLEY RECOLLECTIONS

On a sharp February morning in 1991 Roy Trimble, a quiet man who has lived in and around Belfountain for most of his life, spoke of what it was like to grow up in the Credit Valley. He is perhaps one of the best sources of oral history for the area, certainly one of the most fascinating.

As a boy, he travelled from town to town as his father's employment took him through the Credit system. "We lived in Alton for a while. It seems that Dodds set up a mill in Erin. Dad had to run it. There were two floors and Dodds employed twenty-five or thirty girls. Somewhere along the line Dodds asked Council if they would put a sidewalk in from the main street to the building, because the girls were walking in the mud and so on and it wasn't very nice. So Dodds was to meet Council on a certain day. When he came down to meet them, Council had gone away bowling or something to Acton and forgotten about it. Dodds was so upset that he said to my dad, 'Close her down. Give the girls thirty days. If you want we'll set up another floor in the Alton mill.' That was the lower mill. That was it. So we went to Alton.

"From there we went to Cataract and lived above the powerhouse where Deagle ran his station. We were right above the dynamo in the apartment above." With wry understatement he added, "It was kind of noisy.

"In the summertime there was a cottage down the track, and we moved down there. It was quite private, of course. We weren't there too long until the Cataract Electric people took it over.

"From there we moved here to Belfountain. My dad had been putting in a line and seen this blacksmith's shop." (The blacksmith's shop is now an antique shop and post office in the centre of Belfountain.) "He always loved blacksmithing," said Roy, "so we ended up, in the fall of 1924, coming to Belfountain. That was a blacksmith's shop until about 1929, when we began dabbling with cars. Eventually, as the horses went out, the cars came in. In 1932 I had just finished high school and I said to him, why not go in for garage work. We built a section on and ran the garage. When we closed it up we were only a few months shy of being there for fifty years."

As a boy, Roy experienced a childhood right out of the pages of fiction: "We roamed through the bush and the fields. It was interesting coming to Belfountain because it was so rural. We went fishing. We did a lot of fishing. And swimming in the park. I had to help in the blacksmith's shop, sweep floors and build nail boxes. That's where I spent most of my time in the summer holidays, was in the blacksmith's shop.

"There were a lot of cottagers here. The summer population would double. There had been the Wayside Inn, and they took in people from Toronto. When the cottagers came up we had a ball team. The parking lot at the Conservation Area used to be our ball field. That used to be a garden for Mack, but he let it grow in and we grassed it and rolled it and that was our ball field. It was very large, but it served the purpose and was easily accessible."

Over the years Roy has watched Belfountain shift from a tourist town to a village of young commuters interested in preserving both natural and historical heritage. For Roy Trimble, this is a welcome transition, because Roy has been environmentally aware since the days when it was quirky to be environmentally aware. For Roy Trimble, there is hope that what he has long enjoyed will still be there for future generations.

First sign of Fall.

Caledon Ski Club.

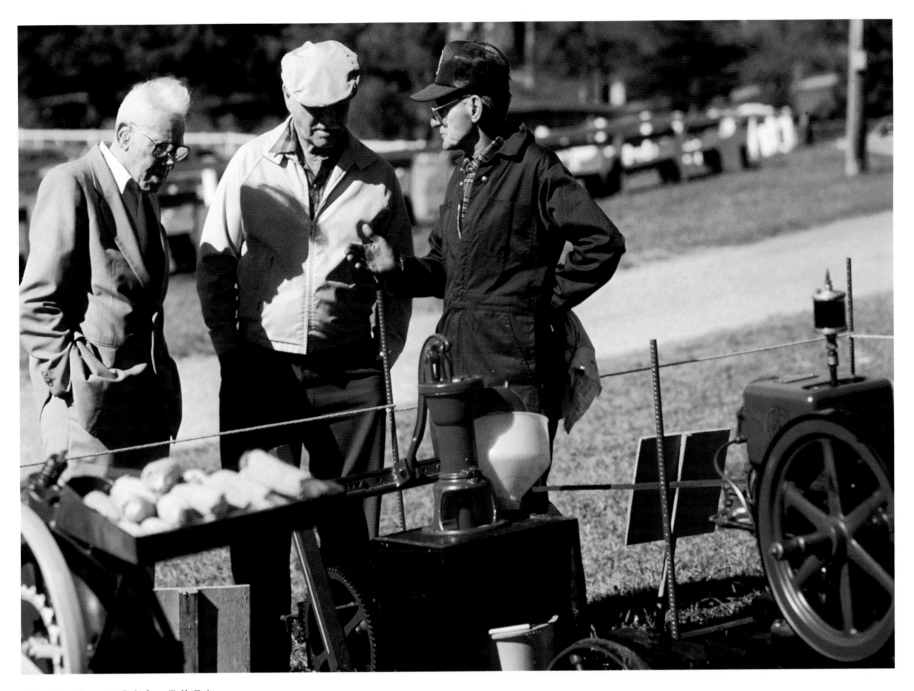

Checking it out, Caledon Fall Fair.

Caledon gravel pits.

Monument to humankind, 5th Line near Terra Cotta.

Cheltenham home.

FROM INGLEWOOD TO CHELTENHAM

South of the towering walls of Caledon Mountain, the Credit River bounces through rolling countryside reminiscent of England's Cotswold Hills. It was the speed of the river and probably the familiar surroundings that caused so many mill towns to spring up in this area. At one time there were as many as sixty-two mills along the Credit's length, all of them with races and millponds — which did much to degrade water quality, destroy salmon runs and diminish water supply.

Inglewood was one of Credit's many mill towns. It bloomed and flourished over a period of twenty years, probably starting sometime around the 1830s, founded by United Empire Loyalists and known then as Riverdale. Many of the Loyalists who settled here, and who operated mills here, were of Yorkshire background and knowledgeable about the technology of the textile industry. In 1843 Thomas Corbett built a dam and the Riverdale Woollen Mill. He later added a carding mill, and a sawmill was soon established. Lumber from the mill and stone from the quarries were hauled to hurly-burly Toronto for the building of docks and breakwaters.

Quarries were established in 1875 by Joachim Hagerman, and later Reid and MacFarlane of Toronto. Besides its use as a building material for breakwaters, much of the stone quarried from Inglewood was employed in the construction of Toronto's curbstones and eccentric Sir Henry Mill Pellatt's mansion, Casa Loma.

Two Ancaster men named Ward and Algie found themselves drawn to Inglewood, and in 1880 they began manufacturing full cloth, flannel blankets, yard goods and underwear, which were then shipped to Cheltenham, Orangeville and Brampton by stage, and later by the Hamilton & Northwestern rail line, which chugged through in 1877.

As the rails opened up the interior, it was thought that Inglewood would flourish. But that vision came to a screeching halt in 1879 when two landowners held up construction of the Credit Valley Railway by demanding full payment for the right of way through their lands. By 1890 Inglewood was still a scattered settlement with a population of only forty people. Today it is probably best known as the home of skier Laurie Graham, whose family owns one of the original stone mills.

Boston Mills was yet another Credit Valley mill town. Named for an old song, "The Road to Boston," Boston Mills was first established by two young Welshmen, David and John Williams, around 1821. The old Boston Mills cemetery, where David is buried, dates back to 1823.

Other settlers came to Boston Mills, cleared the land and raised families. By 1833 a schoolhouse was erected. The village also had a distillery, a tailor who later became the postmaster, and an organ maker.

The mills of Boston Mills weren't established until around 1850, when Hiram Caslor is believed to have built the first sawmill. Prosperity allowed Caslor to open a carding mill, and in 1860 he erected a grist mill, but not without problems. Caslor, it seems, underestimated building costs and fell short by $200 — a sizable sum in those days. Mrs. Caslor, a thrifty woman, slipped into a back room and returned to her despondent husband with a stocking full of coins that would finance the added cost of the mill.

The mills changed hands several times and at one point

Cheltenham Country Store.

were under the guidance of Bracken and Thurston, who installed a roller system for milling grain. The Bracken family eventually took over completely and were the final owners of the mills. Boston Mills became so prosperous that it even had a grain elevator along the Hamilton & Northwestern Railway line and a hotel to service visitors.

However, Inglewood soon began to outpace Boston Mills due to its location at the junction of the Credit Valley and Hamilton & Northwestern railways. As a result, Boston Mills subsided, then fell in a final gasp when the flour mills were razed. The hotel closed in 1884. Around the same time the grain elevator was destroyed and little was left of the village.

The dam, however, remained and was used by Shale Products Limited, where a dynamo was installed to generate electricity for their Inglewood plant. Shale Products was later purchased by the Cataract Light and Power Company. The dam ended in 1931 when it was washed out during flood season, a frequent problem of those days. Today the Boston Mills Antique Shop on Chinguacousy Road is all that's left of the formerly thriving village. It is situated on property that once belonged to the old mills.

Unlike most settlement towns, Cheltenham didn't develop in grid fashion. The Credit River flowed through the land, the Niagara Escarpment rose steeply from the valley, and all attempts to tame the area failed. So Cheltenham just sort of grew — a little here, a little there — sprawling in an easy manner.

Charles Haines, a millwright from Cheltenham, England, came to the area in 1820 and was the founder of the village of Cheltenham. By 1827 his grist mill was in operation, and that industry remained key until 1945, when the mill burned down.

The years 1827 to 1850 were ones of growth and excitement for Cheltenham. From 1850 to 1890 Cheltenham enjoyed its prosperity, bolstered by the railways. Three hotels thrived here. Two distilleries were supported by a number of taverns. There was a steam tannery beside the river, a wagonmaker and a blacksmith. A brickworks went into production in 1871, and in the early 1900s a large deposit of Medina shale was discovered and the Interprovincial Brick Company was born. Thirteen houses were built at the brickyards and rented to workers for between $8 and $13 a month. Seasonal help was brought in from Terra Cotta and Cheltenham. But by 1950 all this industry had passed and the town became dormant. In 1855 Henry Tucker initiated the development of the village that eventually became Terra Cotta. Attracted by the Credit's excellent and relatively constant flow, he built a grist mill and later added a sawmill. As Tucker was responsible for the guarantee of the mill-seat, it follows that the village became known as Tucker's Mill.

Janet Plewes and her family were the next catalysts of the village. Under her son, Simon, the family took over the mills and the settlement became known as Plewes' Mills.

By 1866 the village was more frequently referred to as Salmonville, because of the profusion of salmon in the Credit River. It could now boast a hotel, inn, general store, post office and Methodist Church. The village continued to grow, boosted by the Hamilton & Northwestern Railway, and soon had a forge and carriage shop, a telegraph office and another grist mill.

However, by the time the village came to be known as Terra Cotta (meaning baked earth), a decline had set in. Overfarming had depleted the soil's nutrients and many businesses had closed. A brickworks flourished here under the Plewes, taking advantage of the red clay, but this business also failed. After a series of rejuvenations and declines, the Great Depression hit the village, closing the brickyards, and Terra Cotta subsided for a time.

There is a legend of a ghost at Plewes' mill. It seems the Plewes' night-watchman often saw a white apparition drift through the mill. Not to be subdued, he stalked the spirit with a double-barrelled shotgun. One night when the spirit appeared from under the mill wheel, the watchman accosted it. The ghost, however, turned out to be a real flesh-and-blood man who wanted to buy the mill. The apparition thought he could negotiate a more attractive selling price by creating enough superstition that no one else would want to buy the establishment.

After 1948, with the ravages of the Depression and the war diminishing, Rod Clancy operated a recreation park just outside the village, complete with ten cottages and a pond. The business was sold to Leo Wolf and Gordon Warner in 1952. Six years later it came under the auspices of the Credit Valley Conservation Authority.

The Conservation Area is a Niagara Escarpment Natural Environment park consisting of 160 hectares with multi-use recreational facilities. It is one of the ten nodal parks along the Escarpment. In many places the ancient red Queenston shale is evident along the river beds. Springs feed the Credit River from groundwater that also flows into five man-made ponds in the day-use area. Muskrat Pond and Wolf Lake are also spring-fed.

At one time the area was home to black bears, lynx, fishers, wolverines and elk, but as settlement occurred and habitat was destroyed, these animals were driven out. Today, if you're quiet and careful, you may still see deer, mink or great blue heron.

Boston Mills Cemetery.

Terra Cotta.

The Forge, Terra Cotta.

Taking a hike at the Terra Cotta Conservation Area.

The Credit River, Terra Cotta.

Wind and water erosion have created these spectacular badlands in Caledon near Terra Cotta.

Crazy Boat Race, Credit River at Terra Cotta.

Glen Williams area view of Georgetown.

DESCENDING THE ESCARPMENT

In the area just below the Escarpment where the Credit begins to broaden lies a village known as Glen Williams, named for the glen's first real settler, Benajah Williams, who fathered fifteen children. One member of his family, Charles Williams, was responsible for establishing a sawmill and, by the 1860s, flour and woollen mills. A man of great ambition, Benajah became the justice of the peace and was known locally as Squire Williams (whether in respect or derision is unclear).

Fire, the nemesis of so many early settlements, damaged the sawmill and a brick store, and destroyed the local rake factory. The sawmill was rebuilt in 1877, with a capacity to run 14,000 board feet of lumber per day. This was high production.

A second sawmill was built in the 1850s by Joseph Tweddle. It was sold in 1872 and used as a shoddy mill. Shoddy is a material made from shredded rags and new wool. (Despite the settlers' propensity for consuming the natural landscape, they did know a great deal about thrift and recycling.)

The third sawmill, a steam-driven technological wonder, ran above the Escarpment but burned in 1876.

As Charles Williams became involved in other activities, his son, Joseph, took over the operation of the sawmill and later sold it to H.P. Lawson of Georgetown. This very mill became a source of electricity, first from a water-driven generator and later driven by steam. It provided power to the Georgetown Electric Light and Power Company.

The woollen mill established by Benajah's son Jacob in 1839 burned in 1867. Disaster continued to plague Jacob. During the construction of a new stone mill, one of the beams broke, killing three workers and injuring many others. This mill also burned, but undaunted, Jacob built a

bigger and better version, employing fifty to sixty workers.

However, by 1878 Jacob was experiencing financial difficulties and he put the mill on the market. By 1907 it had become the Glen Woollen Mills Company Limited, and at the same time a subsidiary was started, the Melrose Knitting Company, where wool socks were made. This sock company employed sixty to seventy people and could have employed as many as a hundred if labourers had been available. The company ended abruptly when the mill burned in 1954.

Glen Williams was eventually absorbed by Georgetown, and most indicators that this was once an independent community are now gone.

West of the Credit River, along Black Creek, shimmers Fairy Lake, and over this small lake loom the hulking remains of a tannery and Acton's main commercial attraction, the Olde Hide House.

Situated on one of the main tributaries of the Credit, Acton was first settled by Silas Emes in 1829. Emes was probably a surveyor who was given land as part of his pay. Like most surveyors, Emes didn't stay long on his holdings. In 1834 he was followed by Esia Adams, the forefather of the real developers of what became the town of Acton.

When the first grocery store was established by Wheeler Green, the settlement came to be known as Danville, after a young clerk named Dan who worked there. After the Adamses had established themselves as the town's primary developers, and because the family held the mill-seat, the name of the settlement changed to Adamsville. The family's first mill was located on the site of the present-day feed mill.

Acton's present name wasn't established until 1844, when

Antique barn at Glen Williams.

the postmaster, Robert Swan, was required to register a name for government records. From then until 1873, when Acton became an incorporated village, the hamlet was a part of the Township of Esquesing.

In 1840 A. Nellis established a tannery here. The tannery burned in 1852 but was rebuilt by a man named McKay, who soon sold the business to Atcheson, McGlashon and Co. The tannery was sold again in 1865, this time to the Beardmore family. Fire destroyed the buildings again in 1872, but Beardmore, determined to stay in business, rebuilt on the same foundations. The tannery remained in the Beardmore family until 1944.

Acton's prosperity could be linked directly to the success and failure of the tannery, which ran until 1986 and employed many of the town's people. In 1976 it was reported to be one of the largest tanneries in the British Empire. By 1986, however, Canada Packers Inc. held the controlling interest, and in an effort to consolidate this operation with one in Aurora, the Acton division was closed, putting 329 people out of work. At the time, the division was experiencing economic setbacks directly attributable to the removal of import quotas and the high cost of environmental controls. The tannery's buildings are still in existence, covering 228,600 square metres on 191 hectares. In fact, the Olde Hide House uses one of the old Beardmore warehouses.

A triangle of land downstream of Acton and bordered by the Credit River and Silver Creek was once a hallowed region where the Neutrals, an Iroquoian-speaking people, buried their dead. Burial rites were long and grim by our standards. A body was kept in a cabin until it lost all resemblance to its human form, presumably to allow the spirit to totally abandon its flesh. Then, and only then, the body would be interred in a burial mound. The men were buried in a ring of mounds that surrounded the women, who were buried in the centre.

When the area finally opened to white settlement, around the 1820s, George Kennedy and his wife, Elizabeth, made their way to a place then known as Hungry Hollow. Kennedy had purchased 81 hectares of land for 5 shillings. This land was on the present-day site of Caruso's Fruit Market. It was Kennedy's dream to build a community, and understanding that no community could exist without mills, he established a grist mill at the foot of present-day Mill Street, opening his home overnight to the farmers who came to use his services. Kennedy went on to establish a sawmill and a foundry.

Much to Kennedy's dismay, however, the growth of Hungry Hollow was slow. Enter the Barber brothers. They arrived in 1837, purchased land from Kennedy and proceeded to establish more mills. By 1846 Hungry Hollow's population had grown to an overwhelming 300 and it had been renamed Georgetown, in honour of its founder. A Methodist church had been built and there was a general store, owned by John Sumpter. The following year it was decided that the town's children needed education, and a school was established.

There was no turning back now. Surrounded by prime, arable land, serviced by a booming mill trade because of the Credit River, and close to good shipping, Georgetown exploded to 1,200 people by 1864 and applied for incorporation as a village. By this time the Barber brothers had become the driving force behind Georgetown. Their wallpaper business is reported to have been the largest manufacturer of wallpaper in North America. In 1880 their paper mill became the first electric-powered paper mill in the world. Energy for this mill was transmitted from a dynamo 3 kilometres downstream.

Established in 1843, the Dayfoot Tannery operated until 1947. It employed fifty men and distributed its products as far west as the Pacific coast. Another tannery, the Hillock, was destroyed by fire in 1876.

All of this industry was complemented by hotels, potters, carriage works and other services attendant to a flourishing community. The town's first newspaper, the *Georgetown Herald*, churned out its premier issue in 1866 and remained in continuous production until February 1992.

As the mills and tanneries died out, Georgetown diversified its economic base sufficiently and today continues to be a thriving centre.

The settlement of Norval began around the same time as Georgetown, in the 1820s, when James Macnab, son of a United Empire Loyalist who had fled from the United States, developed a mill on the Credit River and called his embryonic village Esquesing Mills. Macnab extolled the virtues of his mills and encouraged tradesmen to come and settle in his village. But all did not go according to plan. By 1830 Macnab had fallen into financial difficulty and had to lease out his mills to John Barnhart, then to sell them to Peter Adamson in 1838. Adamson had been a colonel in the Portuguese army and had fought many battles with Wellington against Napoleon. There was a sense of grandeur about the Adamson blood, and the family soon became known up and down the Credit River as ambitious entrepreneurs. They did not have that reputation in Esquesing Mills, however. By 1845 Peter Adamson had leased the mills to Gooderham.

The name Esquesing Mills was to be tossed out in favour of Norval when the post office was established.

Halloween at Cedar Sands Farm.

In addition to the economic difficulties experienced by Norval's mills, the community was dealt another blow. The Grand Trunk Railway, which finally came through the area in 1853, by-passed Norval 2 kilometres to the north. Wheat production was the major industry in the mid-1800s, and farmers needed access to affordable shipping. Georgetown was to take what Norval could not.

Yet Norval continued to eke out an existence. By the 1860s, flax was the area's primary crop, and so a flax mill was built to accommodate that market. When that market collapsed, the mill was refitted as a carding mill in 1878.

The Glen Williams, Georgetown and Norval areas survive today with agriculture as a most important industry, but it is an industry under seige. While the surrounding land remains some of the best farmland in Ontario, world trade conditions and consumer trends are challenging, indeed jeopardizing, this most basic of industries.

Old limestone quarry near Limehouse.

Scotsdale Farm, Trafalgar Road north of Georgetown.

Farm near Halton Hills, 9th Line.

In the clouds, Halton Hills, 9th Line.

Georgetown.

Georgetown Highland Games.

Heritage Road, Brampton.

THE FRESH NEW FACE OF FARMING

Located on Heritage Road about 2 kilometres south of Highway 7 is a heritage farm that has been in the Laidlaw family for five generations. It was cleared in 1832 by a Laidlaw, 202 hectares of virgin forest on the rich Peel Plain that rolled away from the broadening Credit River, land covered in maple, white pine and ash. There were bears on the land. There were coyotes. Fish ran the river and the herons followed them. It was a land of fullness and a land of fear. This was the backwoods. But if you were an exiled United Empire Loyalist you took what the land offered and tamed what it didn't.

Steve Laidlaw, a fifth-generation grandson of that original Laidlaw, still works the land his distant forefather cleared. The end is still the same, a matter of survival, but the means have changed remarkably, and the founding farmer would be bewildered by what his great-great-great-grandson is doing to the face of agriculture. It's called Pick-Your-Own.

Faced with rising taxes, rising costs, and a market price that hasn't increased since the 1970s, it is an option that many farmers are trying. The reason is simple: Pick-your-own farming gives control back to the farmer. It eliminates the middleman. It puts profits directly into the farmers' pockets and allows them to once again take the lion's share of the return for the lion's share of the labour.

Steve had been running a revamped dairy farm, some of it on rented property in Erin Mills and Mississauga. "We hit a growing pain, or crunch, in the 1970s, in that we couldn't afford to buy land," Steve explains. "It got very expensive. We couldn't expand the farms the way the farms have always expanded around here: As a son came along you bought the boy another farm — which is why there are seven or eight Laidlaw farms along this road and hidden away on sideroads. We were having trouble with labour at that time. Suddenly nine dollars an hour wasn't cutting it for a hired man. So we went out of dairy. We had about ten acres [4 hectares] of orchard about that time, and we planted another sixty acres [24 hectares] of orchard with the idea that we would supply the chain stores. We built a packing house. We already had some cold storages which were built in the 50s. So we packed for the chain stores for about ten years. During that period these trees were growing."

For a change, the Laidlaws' hilly, fertile land worked in their favour. Steve says, "It's worked for pick-your-own because there's wonderful scenery back here in the fall. All this valley lights right up with colour. That's what pick-your-own is all about. You're selling sight, sound and smell. Apples are fine — yes, we have seventeen types — but what you're really selling is this wonderful wagon ride back along the valley, where we grow strawberries and corn both sides of the Credit. It makes our farm very, very scenic."

Steve sees a trend toward entertainment in farming. "There are five farms near Chicago doing pumpkin theme parks," he says. "They're making a lot of money. What they're doing is the haunted barn and the haunted house and the haunted pumpkin patch. They're only open for one month of the year, selling pick-your-own pumpkins by the pound. There are two now in Ontario, selling pumpkins at twenty-nine cents a pound. You're paying ten bucks for a pumpkin, a wagon ride, a witch and a ghost who will scare you, because that's fun. And, yes, I'll pay ten dollars for a pumpkin because I've just taken the two kids out and they've had a great time.

Fall apple harvest, Heritage Road.

"These guys are bringing in over five hundred thousand people during thirty days. They're charging two bucks a head at the gate and then two bucks to go through the haunted house. But those farms have survived. They aren't doing the conventional six chickens and thirty cows. They're alive. And they're making money."

It's a good idea, a money-making idea, but like most things to do with nature, impact is slow to occur. With five to eight years' wait until the Laidlaws' new orchard would bear significantly, Steve and his family planted tomatoes, sweet corn and other market produce between the rows of trees. They brought in apples from Georgian Bay to mix with their own small yield, and they developed their market, knowing that their farm's potential would not be realized until the 1980s.

"That worked great," says Steve, "and we packed away for ten years while the orchards were maturing. Just as they were maturing, a thing called pick-your-own came along. The first year we had six cars here and, oh, we were awfully busy, thought we were in complete bedlam. My dad didn't know what to make of it all. And that's how we evolved into pick-your-own — with great planning, a bit of luck, and times changing and us changing with those times."

The Laidlaws have capitalized on a market that was being developed by Tom Chudleigh in Milton and Al Ferry nearby, who both saw the potential of this entertainment agribusiness in the 1960s. The concept has done so well for the Laidlaws that they have expanded into pick-your-own strawberries on 4 hectares in the valley, and 28 hectares of sweet corn. During peak season their enormous parking lot is crammed. People come in droves to experience a lost part of their heritage, to once again touch the land, to let their children come eyeball to eyeball with a nanny goat or a bleating sheep.

Customers buy apples they've picked themselves. They buy corn. They come for the day and savour the luscious taste of strawberries freshly picked. Steve and the other Laidlaws tempt their guests with homemade pies, candy apples, herbs and garden produce. And the guests go home — children and parents, students and teachers — with a better understanding of what it means to live from the land.

It's very much a ma-and-pa operation," Steve admits. "This isn't a major corporation here, but it's allowed us to keep this farm alive. Many farms have died in this area. They've sold for speculation or they just couldn't survive. For these farms to be paved over, yes, it's sad because it's a change, and yes, it is good land, but you can't make a living.

"The farms down the road were bought in 1960. They were the Mississauga farmers. The Mississauga farmers came up the road. In their lifetimes they've actually sold two farms, which is a strange phenomenon. They've made more from selling their farms than they ever have from farming. That's what happened in a number of cases in this area, where the land's now under pressure from development. These farmers went through that in '61 because their farms used to be where Square One is right now. The up side to it is that it's taken twenty years for development to come up this far.

"There's likely going to come a day in my lifetime when they're going to drop enough dollars on the table that I'm going to say, 'What am I doing? There's a limit here. I've done my best. Just make interest in the bank and go fishing — a lot.'"

Yet, like most farmers, Steve finds himself tied to the land. Farming is an integral part of him. He *likes* farming. He explains, however, that there is now a great deal of pressure involved in farming. "It's a young man's game, that's for sure. It's changed from my father's time to my time. You're a mechanic one day, a CA [chartered accountant] the next. You're wearing a lot of hats to try and run a company. And that's really what it is now, but you're doing it with resources that don't allow you two bookkeepers and a secretary, which is really what you need."

But maybe, just maybe, Steve Laidlaw and other likeminded farmers have found a way to once again make farming a viable way of making a living. By diversifying, and by capitalizing on nostalgia and the population's demand for entertainment, farmers in the Credit Valley and similar parts of Canada may be able to keep these heritage farms in their families for another generation.

Someplace Else, Mississauga Road, Huttonville.

Riding the rails, Highway 7 overpass near Georgetown.

A HERITAGE VILLAGE ON THE CREDIT

Historic Meadowvale Village lies tucked against the Credit River along Derry Road. One of Ontario's heritage communities, Meadowvale Village was founded as the result of an exodus of thirty Irish families from New York in 1820. Led by Thomas Graham and John Beatty, the troupe eventually travelled up Dundas Street to the Credit River. There the band broke up, each family heading to their 81-hectare parcel.

For the next four years this group of thirty quiet farms remained just that. Then, in 1824, Evan Richards arrived. A man bent on turning a profit, Richards cleared his inexpensive land and sold it two years later for $875 to Jane Heron. This was the beginning of what could have been called land speculation. Jane Heron sold the same land in 1828 to Matthew Dawson for the grand sum of $3,295. (And we thought our property prices skyrocketed.)

This flurry of real estate deals was Meadowvale's only real business enterprise until 1831, when the last member of the original group of Irish exiles left. That year John Beatty sold his holdings to John Crawford, who subsequently established Meadowvale's first mill. With the establishment of this sawmill, the area now had a reason to open to trade. Such opportunity soon attracted John Simpson, who dammed the Credit for a carding mill and a second sawmill in 1836, the year of Meadowvale's incorporation.

Even with its mills, Meadowvale failed to attract any service industries, and as a result the village found itself unable to maintain self-sufficiency. It remained dependent upon the surrounding agricultural trade, which at that time was mostly in wheat. Wheat boomed for a time, fed by the war effort in the Crimea, and during that period Meadowvale experienced a brief moment of prosperity, expanding to 300 people. When peace was restored, Meadowvale's prosperity collapsed along with wheat prices. The major grist mill, owned by Francis Silverthorne, was forced into bankruptcy and taken over by Gooderham and Worts, who also owned majority shares in the Bank of Upper Canada.

Another blow was dealt when the Grand Trunk Railway, which was supposed to have steamed through Meadowvale, steamed through Brampton instead. Although supported by Gooderham and Worts, Meadowvale was soon outpaced by Brampton, and in 1877, when the Credit Valley Railway finally reached the village, it was too late.

The village continued its decline until it met a challenge to its very existence. When expanded highway systems were deemed necessary, Meadowvale Village was placed under consideration as a third alternative to a northern or southern route. Thanks to the foresight of some intelligent planners, the Ontario Heritage Foundation, and considerable compromise, this historic village is now preserved under a heritage designation. The highway will run through the back of Credit Valley Conservation Authority's property, north of the village.

Credit River near Meadowvale.

Canadian watercolour painter Jack Reid in his Brampton studio.

Brampton Fair.

Churchville Park.

Lionhead Golf & Country Club, Mississauga Road in Brampton.

Fresh tracks, Creditview Road bridge north of Steeles Avenue.

The Credit at Steeles Avenue.

Marching shadows.

FAREWELL, TIMOTHY STREET

Here in the southern lands of the Credit the river almost becomes lost in the sprawl of urban development — fields of new housing developments, commercial strip malls that seem to appear overnight, and then there are the towers of Mississauga that loom just down the horizon.

One of Mississauga's communities is Streetsville, now virtually unrecognizable from its humble beginnings. In 1821 a young man by the name of Timothy Street threw up a frame grist mill with two runs of stones on 128 hectares of land that he was determined to conquer. He purchased the actual mill lands on Christmas Eve from the shrewd Andrew Stewart for the exorbitant sum of £2,000. This was indeed exorbitant, because the whole township had been assessed at £11,348. The amount, however, probably included a loan for the cost of a dam and the buildings, as Street hadn't been compensated for his 1812 war losses of £1,750.

Hailing from an illustrious background of Loyalists who had fought with the King's Royal Regiment, Butler's Rangers and with Joseph Brant's Mohawks at Oriskany, Timothy Street knew a great deal about determination and the need for discipline. With his grist mill established, Street went on to develop a sawmill with the help of his millwright associate, John Embelton. This prompted a buying spree that eventually turned him a tidy profit. Street bought extensive lands through the prime territory of Chinguacousy, and in fact at one time owned most of what is now Huttonville. In 1824 he sold all holding except his Streetsville lands.

What Timothy needed now was an enterprising merchant, which came in the person of Montreal lawyer John Barnhart. Barnhart built a store directly opposite Timothy Street's mill in order to capitalize on trade from the farmers who came to grind their grain. Barnhart built himself a home known as The Headquarters and a trading post called Montreal House, which was situated along Mullet Creek.

Streetsville's new mills and businesses attracted other families to the community. Street went on to found a distillery and tannery, in effect controlling almost all of Streetsville's major industries. In 1825, however, his home burned. Whether his reaction was due to despair or anger or real need is unclear, but one week after the fire Timothy put all his lands up for sale. He sold everything and left for new horizons. In five short years he had built a major centre, made his fortune, and made his exit.

Busy Bee at Bread & Honey Festival.

Salmon jumping during spawning runs in the lower Credit River.

THE SALMON'S RETURN

Just as the upper Credit supports an abundant trout fishery, the lower Credit supports an abundant salmon fishery. Once a major spawning ground for the Atlantic salmon, the Credit's fishery all but died in the early part of this century due to overfishing and pollution.

In 1960 the first phase of a reintroduction plan was implemented when the Credit was stocked with young coho, a top predator. This plan allowed lamprey control to be measured and provided an opportunity to reinstate a sport fishery in Lake Ontario.

The coho did so well that by the 1970s chinook salmon were introduced. Chinook are the largest of the Pacific salmon, averaging 6 to 18 kilograms at maturity, with some recorded specimens surpassing the 50-kilogram mark. Coho are smaller, averaging 3 to 7 kilograms, with some hitting 10 kilograms.

The appearance of pink salmon came as somewhat of a surprise — in fact, it was an excellent example of what carelessness in the environment can do. Luckily, this time the error was a fortuitous one.

In the 1950s the Ministry of Natural Resources experimented with the introduction of pink salmon to Hudson Bay. However, the frigid waters of the bay were not to the liking of the pink salmon, and the experiment failed miserably. A few thousand of the remaining salmon were flushed down a storm sewer in Thunder Bay, and that sewer led into a river that emptied into Lake Superior. These waters were more to the salmon's liking. They subsequently established themselves in parts of Lake Huron and Lake Erie, with scattered small schools in Lake Ontario. Because the Lake Ontario population is so small, pink salmon are uncommon in the Credit River, but they are still present.

All species of Pacific salmon die after spawning, whereas some Atlantic salmon spawn more than once. Due to higher water quality and continued reforestation, the Atlantic salmon are increasing their numbers in the Credit River.

While the Pacific salmon spawn in the lower reaches of the Credit, the Atlantic salmon move upstream as far as Inglewood to spawn. The indigenous Atlantic salmon swim once again in their ancestral waters.

Culinary creations at the Barber House, Mississauga.

Creditview Road and the Credit River.

Traffic on the 403, Mississauga.

The Culham Trail.

Burnhamthorpe Road bridge.

Fall colours, Erindale Park, facing St. Peter's Anglican Church.

ERINDALE AND DUNDAS STREET

John Graves Simcoe, commander of the Queen's Rangers in the American Revolution and newly appointed governor of Upper Canada, arrived at his posting in 1792. Being a military man, it didn't take him long to realize that the two native paths that crossed the Credit, one near Erindale and the other near the river's mouth, were a direct link between Kingston, Niagara and Detroit. He immediately set about to build a road over these paths. If hostilities with the Americans recurred, such a road would permit easy movement of British troops.

By 1793 he had the first section of Dundas Street opened as a portage road for wagons between Lake Ontario and the Upper Thames. York to Burlington Beach was marked by 1794, following the old inland route. A sleigh and bridle path was opened by Augustus Jones and the Queen's Rangers in 1796, and this was improved to a wagon road by 1798, when Lakeshore Road opened. The inland road, however, was used more frequently because the upper streams could be forded when the southern bridges were washed out.

Roads by themselves weren't enough. Simcoe realized that couriers would need refreshment and accommodation on these long journeys, and he planned a series of inns for Dundas Street. One of these was to be situated at the spot where Dundas Street met the Credit River. But it wasn't until 1798, after Simcoe had left Upper Canada, that this plan finally came to fruition. The inn was called Government House. It was large for the time period, a 12-by-9-metre construction of squared timbers, operated by Col. William Allan, J.P., a prominent merchant in York.

By 1802 most of the lands north of Lake Ontario had come under treaty, and those that hadn't did so by 1818. In return, the British, in their magnanimity, allowed the Mississaugas to retain the land that is now the Mississauga Golf Club.

Settlers arrived in considerable numbers, many having received land grants. It was all part of a military strategy: A peopled territory with logical, accessible roads for troop movement is a difficult territory to invade. With increasing demand for homestead lands, the reserve area retained by the Mississaugas was sold off in three blocks. The centre block, which straddled Dundas Street, was sold for road allowance and surveyed into lots, then sold to James McGill, who owned mills on the Credit. McGill was required to retain 15 hectares for a town plot.

At that time the settlement was known as Credit or Credit Village, but it soon became Springfield and then Springfield-on-the-Credit.

By 1830 the village lots had been purchased, the streets named, and a general store had sprung into operation. This was followed by a chairmaking factory and a knitting mill, which ran on a burned-out sawmill site owned and operated by Joe Featherston and Emerson Taylor, a cousin of Phineas Taylor Barnum of Barnum and Bailey Circus fame. Taylor eventually bought the Exchange Hotel, which was said to be the finest hotel in Peel County.

No decent community would have been complete without a church, and so Peter and Joseph Adamson, William Thompson, Frederick Jarvis, Alexander Proudfoot and Henry Carpenter purchased land for 10 shillings with the intent of building that church. With labour provided by parishoners,

Winter wonderland at Erindale Park off Dundas Street, Mississauga.

the church was completed by 1827. It was a white clapboard building with a steeple and spire. This structure was later demolished and a brick church was built to replace the wooden one. The spire, added in 1910, was encased with copper in 1949. St. Peter's is still in operation today and is one of the oldest operating churches in the Credit Valley.

Dundas Street opened, and by 1836 a toll had been placed upon road use, to help pay for this major military expense and to assist in the road's maintenance. To cross the Credit bridge cost 10 cents — a stiff toll considering the cost of living in those days. Residents weren't too thrilled with this fee and in a fit of pique, someone blew up the gatekeeper's hut. In response, the gatekeeper closed the bridge. Enough was enough. Completely outraged, the village folk tarred and feathered the fellow.

Prosperity seemed to be in hand for the village by 1877. Dundas Street had been gravelled. Daily stagecoaches from York operated six days a week, with a fee of 2 shillings and sixpence. The population had expanded to 200. Two knitting mills now operated here, employing fifty to sixty people. Mail, however, was another matter. By 1890, with residents' mail constantly being sent to another Springfield, the settlement's name was changed to Erindale.

The advent of hydro further improved Erindale's prosperity, and in 1910 a power dam was completed, with Erindale Hydro supplying electricity for its own community. It seems that hydro was in great abundance, as power was even supplied for lights around an outdoor hockey rink.

Dundas Street was paved in 1924, an event that heralded the community's first traffic problems. Drivers of those obnoxious motor vehicles, out on a Sunday drive, were reported to have been clocked speeding at rates reaching 61 k.p.h. What was the world coming to?

As Erindale and the surrounding urban centres grew, they sprawled into the other, and in 1968 Erindale was incorporated into Mississauga.

Morning commuters, GO Transit near Erindale Station.

University of Toronto, Erindale campus.

Canada Day, Mississauga City Hall.

Looking back on time,
Mississauga City Hall clock tower.

Mississauga Chinatown Dundas Street near Cawthra.

Mississauga downtown reflections.

Graduation congratulations.

THE OLD BRITANNIA SCHOOLHOUSE

In settlement days a schoolhouse signified prosperity, because the number of children grew in direct relationship to the influx of settlers and to their belief in the economic future of their community. In these early one-room schoolhouses, students from grades one through eight were instructed in all of the basic academic subjects.

S.S. No. 12 in Toronto Township was one such school. It was preceded by an earlier wooden schoolhouse erected in 1834 through the largess of King William IV, who granted 82 hectares for the sole purpose of educating his colonial subjects. When the wooden building fell into disrepair, the school trustees decided that a brick structure was in order and had the old building demolished. S.S. No. 12 was built as a common school in 1852.

By 1871 common schools had been gathered under the jurisdiction of the public school system. The prohibitively high fees for attending public schools were abolished and an annual four months of attendance became compulsory for children ages seven to twelve.

In 1959 there came a radical new theory that if children were bussed to a larger central school with individual classrooms for separate grades, it would not only serve to better educate these children but would also reduce overhead. And so S.S. No. 12 closed.

With 82 hectares to maintain and an existing schoolhouse in place, in 1987 the Peel Board of Education began a field studies program whereby children would have an opportunity to not only learn about the past but also to appreciate rural life. Lessons at the schoolhouse are instructed in the nineteenth-century manner. To complement this rural educational experience, the Peel Board of Education has restored an original farmstead, including a milk house, a chicken shed, an icehouse, a corn crib, a smokehouse, a windmill and a drive shed.

Dunton House, which was moved to and reconstructed on the site, was built around 1840 and has received historic designation. Like Dunton House, Conover Barn was also dismantled, transported and reconstructed. The remainder of the lands comprise fields, pastures and forests, as well as a sugar bush where children may pursue environmental, agricultural and historical studies. When completed in 1993, Britannia School Farm will provide unique learning opportunities in almost every subject area.

The Bradley House Museum, Mississauga.

LORNE PARK

Nestled like a dream within the city of Mississauga are the remains of the village of Lorne Park. For centuries the area was used by the Mississaugas, primarily in the fall, when the salmon would run. By the eighteenth century, French and English traders had made their way up through the Great Lakes to trade with the natives. The Mississaugas came to call the river Mess-sin-ni-ke, "a trusting river," which also had the connotation "a river of credit."

The Europeans soon called the river the Credit, but all links between the concepts of trade, trust and credit quickly degenerated. In 1805, at the mouth of the Credit River, eight Mississauga chiefs negotiated with five government officials to transfer land and fishing rights to the British. It was probably the most successful and bloodless occupation that has ever taken place.

The first survey of the area was undertaken in 1806 and the first applicant for land was Moses Polley, who set up a store at the mouth of the Credit.

Lorne Park's origins began when, in 1833, Lieutenant Arthur Jones took ownership of land south of Dundas Street. Jones sold within a year to Frederick Chase Capreol, and it was under Capreol that plans to dam the Credit and build an industrial area along the river formed, and failed. Unable to raise sufficient financing, Capreol sold in 1839. Had he been successful, it is likely that the lovely estates of Lorne Park might instead have been an industrial wasteland.

Between 1839 and 1878 the Lorne Park lands were sold and resold approximately ten times, until finally, in 1878, an investment group purchased the lands with the intention of putting in a resort area complete with a wharf and picnic and refreshment pavilions. The park opened for business on May 24, 1879. The name Lorne Park was allegedly in honour of then Governor General the Marquis of Lorne, who was to have opened the park.

Lorne Park did very well for its investors. Steamer and rail excursions regularly departed from the park and it seemed that prosperity was assured. However, one year later the association was sued for mortgage default and unpaid contractors' bills.

John W. Stockwell and partner were the next to assume ownership of the resort. In 1886 Stockwell took title and created the Toronto and Lorne Park Summer Resort Company. It took Stockwell only two years to subdivide seventy-two lots for homes, with the intention of creating a respectable community. The sale of each lot included stipulations that required the purchaser to build a "neat and respectable cottage or house costing not less than £400. No animals nor fowl shall be kept, no intoxicating or spiritual liquors used except for medicinal purposes, and all water closets and privy pits to be approved by the company." This was to be a place of quiet, dignified living, with north-south streets named after poets and east-west streets after the original company's owners.

Between 1886 and 1891, twenty-seven cottages were erected,

Lorne Park.

Toronto city view.

some of which are still occupied today. Many of these were designed by Edmund Burke, the architect who designed the Simpsons building on Queen Street in Toronto. These cottages were in fact spacious two-storey summer residences with large verandas.

When the wharf collapsed due to decay in 1903, everyone on the dock was rescued, but many purses were lost in the water, and today old coins occasionally wash up on the beach. Attempts to repair the wharf were unsuccessful and it was abandoned. At low water levels the remains of the wharf can still be seen.

With the wharf gone, Lorne Park transformed into a private summer resort where walks, bowling, tennis and other civilized pastimes could be pursued. Ownership passed into the hands of the Lakeshore Country Club from 1909 to 1910. During the same period another association, the Cottages Association, was formed by cottage owners with the intent of overseeing the care of properties. This group went on to form the Lorne Park Club, complete with clubhouses. The association was dissolved around 1934.

Today Lorne Park remains a nostalgic island within Mississauga, a sanctuary for virgin pines and a living reminder of by-gone days.

PORT CREDIT AND THE MISSISSAUGA NATION

A storm blew up on Lake Ontario. An order had been given to come ashore, and struggling, the men of the Queen's Rangers heaved on the oars, bringing Lieutenant Governor John Graves Simcoe to land in the mouth of the Credit River. Soaked from the rain and the waves, Simcoe may have found himself captivated by the sheltered harbour of the Credit, and perhaps it was his wish to be under a warm roof that caused him to suggest an inn be built on this site.

That very inn was completed in 1798, a one-and-a-half-storey squared-timber structure with a stone hearth and chimney quarried from the Credit River and Lake Ontario. This was Government House, and it was to be around the activity of this inn that a settlement would grow.

Management of the inn passed through several hands. In 1805 Thomas Ingersoll, father of Laura Secord, leased Government House for a period of seven years. During that same year the invasion of the interior began. The Credit Council Ring was held between five Crown representatives and eight Mississauga chiefs. A total of 3,238 hectares were forfeited by the natives in exchange for goods and credit worth £1,000. The lands included the lakeshore to a depth of 9 kilometres inland. The British allowed the Mississaugas to continue to fish the waters of Twelve Mile and Sixteen Mile creeks, and the Etobicoke and Credit rivers, while retaining 2 kilometres of land on each side of the Credit. The Mississauga Tract was divided into Toronto, Trafalgar and Nelson townships.

It wasn't long before Government House welcomed the area's first surveyor, Samuel Wilmot. To Wilmot, the sight of an inn plunked within a forest of interminable density would have been nothing new. However, to many of the settlers who sheltered at Government House while building their shanties, this must have seemed a forbidding land — folktales of the evils of forests had long been popular in Europe.

The years between 1805 and 1812 were ones of struggle, excitement and determination for the settlers. For the Mississaugas, it was quite another story. They were now subject to European diseases, invasion, and a radical change of life that would eventually spell the destruction of their nation. In 1812 war was to preoccupy the minds of both the settlers and the Mississaugas. Loyalist and immigrant men marched off to York in droves to serve in the militia. The women, as was to become more and more common, were left to run these backwoods farms on their own. Many of these women had long been accustomed to the life of a lady, but they soon learned to dirty their hands, to suffer the aches of back-breaking labour, to run a household and farm with thrift and with bull-headed determination.

In the first year of the war the Americans took York and captured its militia. These rural militiamen were not trained fighters and their officers argued among themselves. But the British had an edge that the Americans didn't have, the co-operation of the natives. Were it not for the espionage and guerrilla tactics employed by the natives, Canada might very

Goose tracks.

well have ended up a territory of the United States.

When the war finally ended, the colonization of Upper Canada resumed its frenetic pace. Land grants were given to soldiers as a bonus, and as a beneficiary of that program, Charles Ingersoll left Government House and moved to what is now Ingersoll, Ontario.

Hungry for more land, the British again met with native leaders, this time on the Credit River flats. During these negotiations the Crown obtained the rights to all lands north to Georgian Bay. Members of the Chippewa, Mississauga, Iroquois and other nations were parcelled away onto reservations, told to farm their lands, and then generally ignored.

Along the Credit, native fishing rights were lost to the settlements and their mills. Where once they had camped at the mouth, a busy port settlement now mushroomed.

This wasn't enough for the British. In 1820 they purchased the lower Credit lands from the Mississaugas for the contemptible sum of 12 shillings. In that same year the first bridge was built to span the river near its mouth.

Grist and sawmills further upstream shipped all their goods through Port Credit to York and the major centres beyond. Staves were floated downriver in the spring after being stacked on the river banks all winter, and thus the town of Stavebank received its name. Pines along the lakeshore were cut in a frenzy of activity and shipped back to England for Royal Navy masting.

By 1825 the Mississaugas' suffering had reached such a point that the British decided to build thirty log cabins for them at a site about 1½ kilometres from the mouth of the Credit. These were to be situated on the high west bank, the present site of the Mississauga Country Club. The flats below the village were cultivated for crops with assistance from Egerton Ryerson, who later went on to found the Ontario public school system.

Improvements around Port Credit in 1832 included the construction of a bigger and better bridge, and Lakeshore Road was upgraded from a corduroy road to one packed with dirt to make it smoother. By 1834 the government, in a clear change of thinking, had initiated the Port Credit Harbour Company, fifty percent of which was owned by the Mississaugas. The company began construction of a wharf and warehouses on each bank of the Credit and would levy tolls on goods handled. At the same time, 340 acres on the west bank were surveyed and subdivided into 1¾-acre village lots. One of the first to purchase these lots was John Jones, a Chippewa missionary who attempted to bring the native nations into the British fold. Many of the streets would come to be named after the first purchasers.

Port Credit had grown to such a size that by 1835 a bi-daily stagecoach service was initiated from Toronto to Hamilton along the lakeshore. First-class passage would ensure that you didn't have to walk beside the coach or push when the contraption mired in mud.

By 1837 the wharf and warehouses were completed, providing a place for steamer *Britannia* to stop on her daily trip between Toronto and Hamilton. Also in 1837, meetings of a most rebellious nature were taking place at Government House. These meetings resulted in the posting of a £1,000 reward notice for the capture of journalist and politician William Lyon Mackenzie. On December 7 Loyalists easily defeated Mackenzie's rebels, and Mackenzie fled to the United States.

By the late 1830s the Mississaugas were suffering from disease, alcoholism and the deterioration of their culture. Their numbers were now radically reduced. In 1840 they were relocated to the Grand River Indian Reserve, once again losing their homes and their identities. The Mississaugas eventually became a nation lost to Canada.

By 1846 the population of Port Credit was 150. Four years later it had expanded to 250 and the town was home to a shipyard. Five years after that the first steam train entered Port Credit.

As the port town developed, stone hooking became a thriving industry. Stone hooking was the art of quarrying stone from the lake. This involved a specially built two-masted stoneboat that would anchor close to shore. From there seams were cut into the stone and rakes were used to hook the stone and bring it aboard. Much of this stone was shipped to Toronto for the building trade.

In the years that followed, Port Credit saw the erection of lighthouses and the development of an oil refinery and the St. Lawrence Starch Company. The community's first hydro in 1912, and in 1914 Port Credit's incorporation into a village.

Clarkson Refinery.

Tall tales at Uncle's Angling in Port Credit.

The mouth of the Credit River looking north. Lakeshore Road, the railway lines and the Queen Elizabeth Way all cross the river.

Rowing under the railway bridge in Port Credit.

Port Credit River Festival.

Swans at Rattray Marsh, Mississauga.

RATTRAY MARSH

Near the mouth of the Credit River lies Rattray Marsh. Created by retreating glacial Lake Iroquois, for the past 10,000 years it has acted as a filter for Sheridan Creek. This tranquil and diverse conservation area was nearly lost to development.

Originally opened around 1805 after survey, the property has been held over the years by many landowners, including the Oliphants, Peers, Fudgers and Rattray himself. It was Harris H. Fudger, president of the Robert Simpson Company, who built Barrymede Mansion and developed much of the lands. The gatehouse is still in existence, as is Fudger's son's home, Bexhill House, although both are much altered. In 1945 Colonel James Halliday Rattray purchased the lands.

When Rattray died in 1960, his death marked the beginning of sixteen years of frustrating negotiations on the part of several interest groups, including the Rattray Marsh Preservation Steering Committee, in an attempt to bring all or part of the marsh under protection.

There are approximately 450 species of flora within Rattray's 33 hectares, with a bird population that includes the great egret and the black-crowned night heron.

Although preservation efforts began in 1960, three years were spent chasing red tape and people who still thought that marsh was wasteland, fill it in and put up houses. By 1963 the steering committee had come face to face with that very threat. Headed by M. Neiman, a consortium proposed to develop Rattray Marsh into estates.

Meanwhile, the Credit Valley Conservation Authority had already begun to build its information arsenal by having the University of Toronto conduct ecological studies regarding the present condition of the marsh, as well as possible future repercussions from upstream development.

Despite the report's recommendation for a buffer zone around upstream development, in 1967 Toronto Township Council approved Phase I of the Rattray Park Estates. Barrymede Mansion was put to the torch in an attempt to level it. When Barrymede wouldn't burn, the wrecking ball brought it down and the mansion's remains were shoved into the marsh. In addition, homeowners had been required to sign an agreement of no protest with regard to the development of a marina. Rattray was slowly diminishing.

Finally, in 1971, after a CVCA study, 10 hectares of Rattray Marsh were purchased by the Authority — the very hectares Neiman had planned to develop into a marina — and a strategy to purchase the remaining 23 hectares was being formed.

By this time Clarkson, Cooksville, Erindale, Malton and Meadowvale had amalgated into Mississauga, and it was through this planning board that a recommendation was received to purchase the remaining property of Rattray Marsh for the purpose of preservation. In 1972 nature and Lake Ontario helped matters along.

Rising to its highest level since 1953, Lake Ontario flooded Rattray Marsh, leaving land for the proposed Phase II under several metres of water. This prompted fill regulations to come into effect, which meant that before going further, Neiman would have to obtain permission from the CVCA in order for fill to be placed anywhere in Rattray Marsh.

This good fortune was augmented by the caprice of politics. An election year brought in a spate of new officials who felt it important to preserve wetlands not for the sake

Jack Darling Park along the lakeshore.

of nostalgia, but for the sake of humankind's survival. The new mayor of Mississauga agreed to recommend that the city acquire the remaining Rattray property, by expropriation if necessary, with the proviso that the Rattray Marsh Preservation Steering Committee undertake fund-raising toward the city's share of the purchase price.

When brought before Council, it was resolved that the CVCA should acquire the lands on behalf of the City of Mississauga. In turn, the CVCA offered Neiman $1,050,000, which he declined. The CVCA then began expropriation, to which Neiman made no objections.

Rattray Marsh Conservation Area officially opened in 1975, not only for the benefit of generations of humans to come, but for the ecosystem of which we are but one small part.

This was just one battle in a situation that should have nothing to do with battles. The integrity of the Credit Valley watershed isn't something that should be up for debate. It is an undebatable fact that if we don't preserve our green spaces, we, as a species, will create our own demise.

Fall colours at the Rattray Marsh.

Lighthouse at the mouth of the Credit River, Port Credit.

Bibliography

Acton's Early Days. Acton, Ontario: Acton Free Press, 1939.

Adamson, Jean. *Erindale at the Crook of the Credit.* Erin, Ontario: The Boston Mills Press.

Alton: A Pictorial History. Erin, Ontario: The Boston Mills Press.

Brown, Steven J. *If the Walls Could Talk...* Orangeville, Ontario: Local Architectural Conservancy Advisory Committee, 1988.

Clarkson, Betty. *At the Mouth of the Credit.* Erin, Ontario: The Boston Mills Press, 1977.

Cook, William E. *Cook's History of Inglewood.* Erin, Ontario: The Boston Mills Press, 1975.

Johnston, Baptist. *Credit Valley Conservation Report.* Department of Planning, 1957.

Kortland, Patricia. *Hillsburgh's Heyday.* Erin, Ontario: The Boston Mills Press, 1983.

Lorne Park Estates Historical Board. *A Village Within a City.* Erin, Ontario: The Boston Mills Press, 1980.

Manning, Mary E. *Street: The Man, the Family, the Village.* Streetsville, Ontario: Streetsville Historical Society, 1983.

McCartney, E. Michael. *The Orangeville Reservoir.* Credit Valley Conservation Authority, no date.

McMillan C.J. *Early History of the Township of Erin.* Erin, Ontario: The Boston Mills Press, 1974.

Nelles, Frank. *Cheltenham: A Credit Valley Mill Town.* Erin, Ontario: The Boston Mills Press, 1975.

Peek Back Into Georgetown's Past. Georgetown, Ontario: Centennial Middle School, 1970.

Ruggle, Richard. *Down in the Glen.* The Glen William Cemetery, 1978.

Ruggle, Richard. *Norval on the Credit River.* Press Porcepic, 1973.

Stephens, Lorina. *Niagara Escarpment: Touring the Giant's Rib.* Erin, Ontario: The Boston Mills Press, in press, 1993.

Trimble, Berniece. *Belfountain: Caves, Castles and Quarries.* Erin, Ontario: The Boston Mills Press, 1975.

THE BOSTON MILLS PRESS